BACHELORETTE PARTY COLORING BOOK

NAUGHTY GIRL COLORING

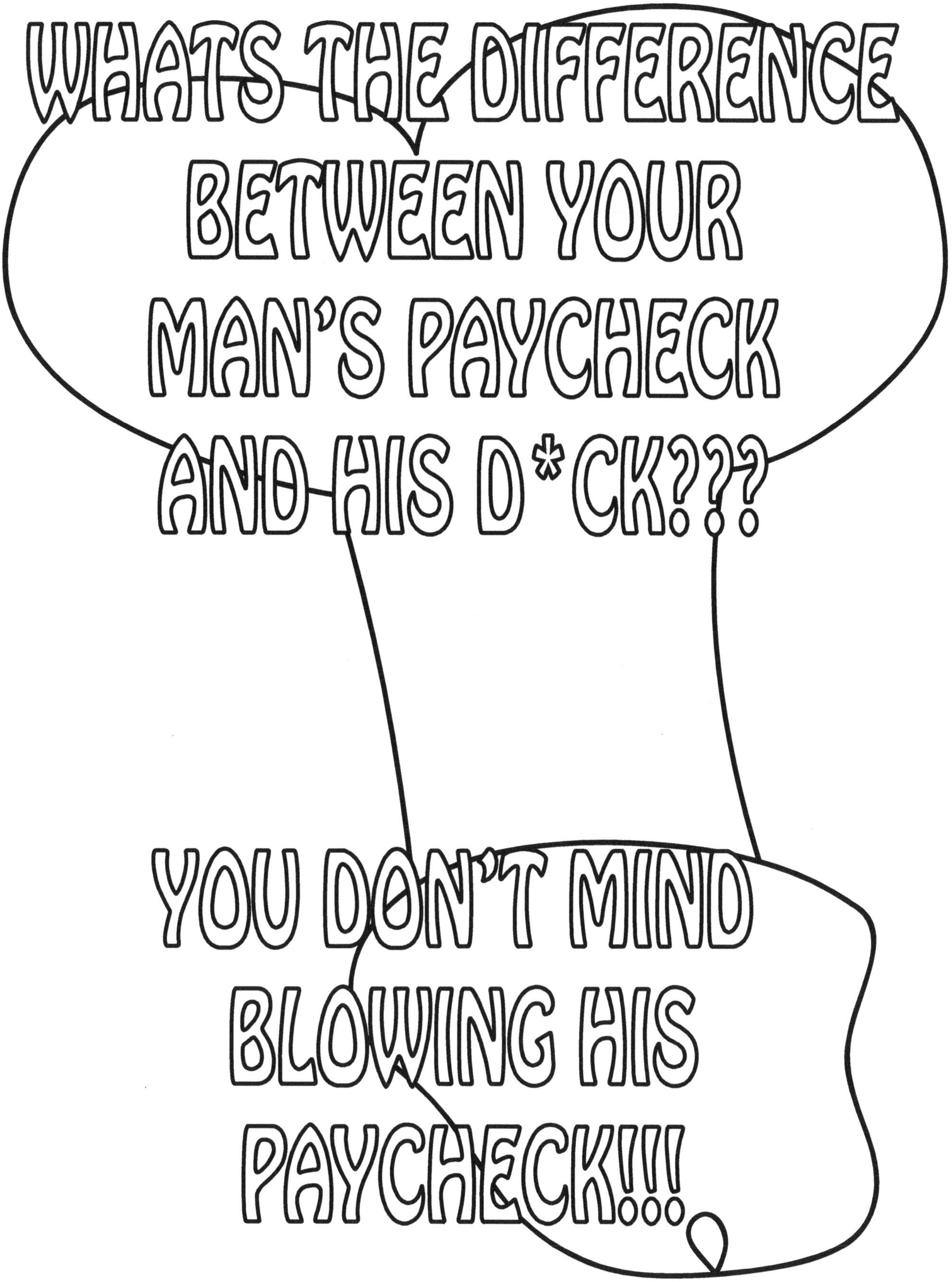
WHATS THE DIFFERENCE
BETWEEN YOUR
MAN'S PAYCHECK
AND HIS D*CK???
YOU DON'T MIND
BLOWING HIS
PAYCHECK!!!

WHAT DO YOU CALL THE USELESS PIECE OF SKIN ATTACHED TO A P*NIS???

A MAN!!!

A MAN ASKS HIS
GIRLFRIEND....
"TELL ME SOMETHING
THAT WILL MAKE ME
HAPPY AND SAD
AT THE SAME TIME!

GIRLFRIEND REPLIES...
"YOU HAVE
A BIGGER P*NIS
THAN YOUR BEST FRIEND!"

THE 3 WORST THINGS ABOUT BEING A DICK HEAD

1, YOUR BEST FRIEND IS A C*NT.

2, YOU LIVE NEXT TO TWO NUTS AND AN ASSH*LE.

3, EVERY TIME YOU GET EXCITED YOU THROW UP.

WHAT'S YOUR FAVORITE D*CK?

HOW IS
A TIGHTROPE WALK
LIKE GETTING
A BLOW JOB FROM SOMEONE UGLY?

IF YOU WANT TO ENJOY
EITHER,
DON'T LOOK DOWN!

SUPER WILLY

SUCCULENT HARD WILLIES.......

FOR LADIES THAT LOVE TO LICK

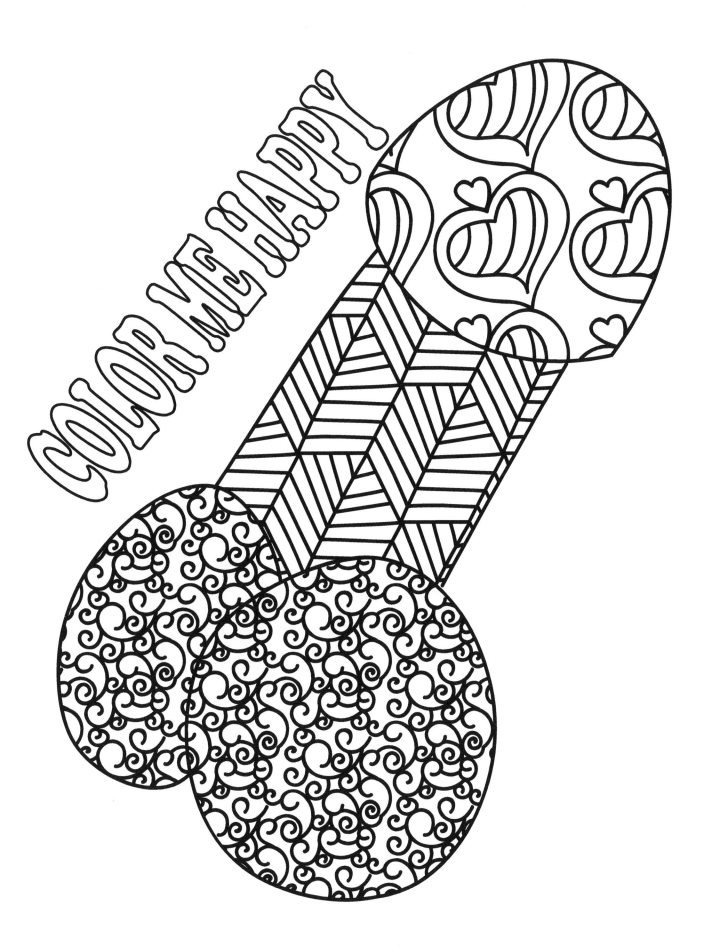

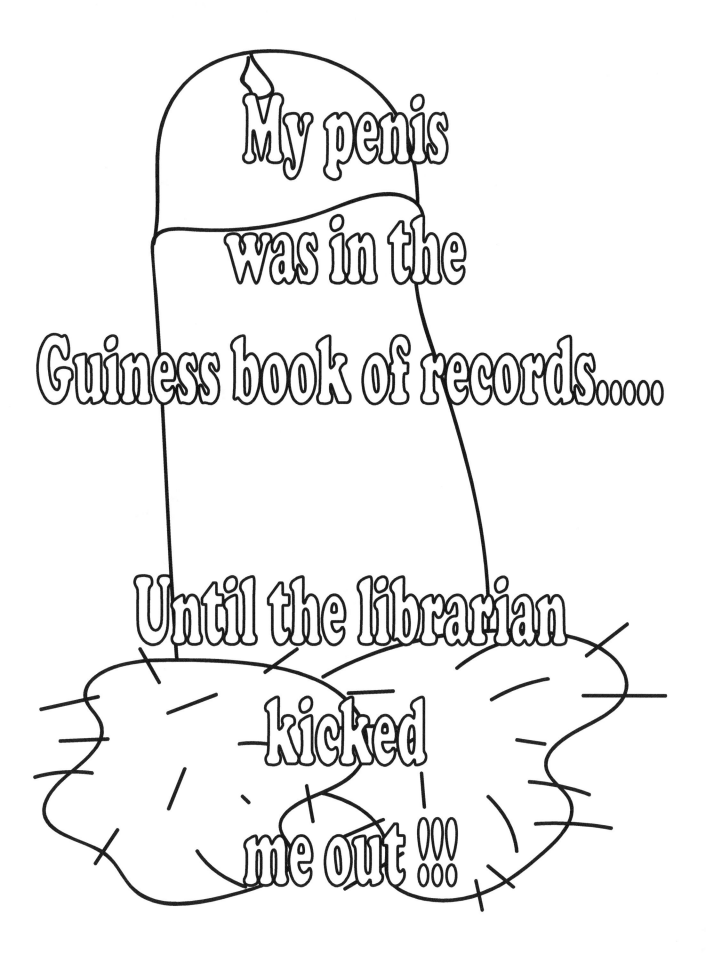

DISSAPOINTMENT....

FINDING

4 INCHES

CPSIA information can be obtained
at www.ICGtesting.com
Printed in the USA
BVHW020751090223
658070BV00019B/90